HOTEL OBLIVION

HOTEL OBLIVION

Cynthia Cruz

Four Way Books
Tribeca

This book is for my mother and my father.

Library of Congress Cataloging-in-Publication Data

Names: Cruz, Cynthia, author.
Title: Hotel Oblivion / Cynthia Cruz.
Description: New York : Four Way Books, [2022]
Identifiers: LCCN 2021047744 | ISBN 9781954245112 (trade paperback) |
ISBN 9781954245198 (epub)
Subjects: LCGFT: Poetry.
Classification: LCC PS3603.R893 H68 2022 | DDC 811/.6--dc23
LC record available at https://lccn.loc.gov/2021047744

Four Way Books is a not-for-profit literary press. We are grateful for the assistance
we receive from individual donors, public arts agencies, and private foundations
including the NEA, NEA Cares, Literary Arts Emergency Fund, and the
New York State Council on the Arts, a state agency.

We are a proud member of the Community of Literary Magazines and Presses.

Contents

oblivion (n.)

late 14c., *oblivioun*, "state or fact of forgetting, forgetfulness, loss of memory," from Old French *oblivion* (13c.) and directly from Latin *oblivionem* (nominative *oblivio)* "forgetfulness; a being forgotten," from *oblivisci* (past participle *oblitus*) "forget," which is of uncertain origin.

The concept of the archive shelters in itself, of course, this memory of the name *arkhē*. But it also *shelters* itself from this memory which it shelters: which comes down to saying also that it forgets it.

—Jacques Derrida, *Archive Fever*

Neukölln

Around the corner
on the river:

three girls in heels.

Crimson, the color
they are saturated in.

Soft gold, its window.

Blood Work—Steady Decline

After Felix Gonzalez-Torres

Have you recently, he asks,
had surgery.

Or an accident, perhaps.

Acute, he says.
His hands miming
catastrophe.

Something
has happened.

In Chinese medicine
they say
the spirit has left the body.

Your spirit, he says,
is floating.

Stammer

There is the story my mother used to tell.
How she woke at 3 a.m.
from a dream that her grandmother died
at 3 a.m.

And when she woke
she learned that her grandmother
died at 3 a.m.

It's like that:
visceral and animal.

The silver grammar of vanish.

A soft violence
pushing up against me—

soundless,
its static,
satelliting music.

Even now, it is there
at the edge, on the periphery.

When I stand in the light before the mirror
it is overpowering.

And always, without end.

Number

Take it in, Genet says.
Drop your body, willing
into the dilation.

Ruined in the apparition
of complex lines and shadows,
wild-weed and rattle of this
black fragment of city park,

Genet.
Loving anyone
who will tender.

Criminal, hopeless,
strange and inside
the brutal fever of this
small strange night: 2 a.m.,
nadir-blue, Eastern city.

Genet, my other, brave
double, tell me,
what do I say, what do I
do—

to the dream

when it comes to me.

Saturday

What is a fragment, a found
postcard, ephemera, ruin or a photograph.
For example: Doris Peter's "Children
collecting scrap metal, George Washington Street,
1997," Russian. Or a Che Guevara montage
on dream board in the sweetshop, Neukölln.
Why glean, why assemble, or
how does accumulation keep.
How does getting it all down
do the same work as making. And how
is the gluing of words together
not unlike taking something beautiful apart.
In the afternoon, on Saturday,
I bought a pale blue dress from Humana
and walked alone, home, in it,
through the parades of my emptiness.

The Ring

I am learning to speak, again.
Astral, spectral, half-in-dream.
I make my way through the jig-
saw of a cruel and perfect grammar.
Or, just barely. And I have stopped
making work that can't disappear.
But the music is too much for me. I can take it
but only in minute and fixed increments.
Baby food in a spoon, measured in bite-fulls,
or a capsule I swallow only in daylight,
midday after classes. I take it, a sweet
obscene ointment, cosmetic, or
medicine. The most nourishing.
Delicate gold capsule of infinite
emollient and sorrow, I swallow
the powder and it enters me.
Like ink spilling, or voracious,
an appetite, and all-consuming.
A memory or a snapshot, its flash-light,
illuminating, it takes me, and then
it erases everything.

Fragment: Pollen

Relentless, the song that keeps me up
every night now for weeks.
The color of crimson, its feel
is rich on the skin, a food-
like substance. But more precise and hopeful.
Secret, it sounds like a murmur,
unrecognizable, just like this:
I bought myself a cream-
colored blouse, French, with tiny shell buttons
and a narrow, black, ribbon-like tie
for survival, a book of Unica Zürn's last letters,
sketches, and ephemera, and a pair of white stockings in dot-
like pattern, like snow in summer,
in Grünwald, or near my neighborhood,
the forest at the precipice near the water
at daybreak. The days here are not
like days at all. But, instead, like a film,
the top layer of dream. The city I am in
is completely different from Brooklyn.
And, also, it is exactly the same.
I'm reading Zürn's final letters to her sister, after
she followed Bellmer to Paris.
Her tiny drawings are exquisite
and intricate like the broken traces

of memory that occur upon waking.
Everything I eat
here tastes the same, like cream-filled
pastries, or warm milk
served in a porcelain cup
to a child unable to sleep,
in the middle of the night.
You confuse yourself, she said,
so you can tell yourself you don't
know. But you do, she said,
you do.

Fragment: Small Talk on Melancholia

In Lars von Trier's film, *Melancholia*, Kirsten Dunst's

character, Justine, tries to keep one step ahead of it.

You can see this in the first half of the film

where, at her own wedding, she keeps moving.

From room to room, guest to guest, through

the many rooms of her sister's mansion

as if moving back in time to her own beginning

until, in the end, she finally collapses. Moving through

rooms and rooms of the mansion like endless

rooms of memory. And what is it

she collapses into? She loses herself inside a kind of small death,

not unlike what happens when one eats sweets, or dreams,

or the moment when an idea enters the mind. Her madness

is no madness, it is a reprieve, a tiny sleep, a space

she forms out of nothing, and then enters, an in-between.

Where do I go when I drop into sleep? Where

does my mind vanish into?

When I tasted the cake I went away for a small moment,

I was erased. I entered something else, a next-to

world. Or, when I leave the body and lose time

in thought. It is the body that leads me,

though I always want to anchor myself in the mind.

Justine wants to leave the world she lives in—

its small rules and hard corners. It isn't death

she envisions, but a tiny collapse, a din to drop into.
Death, or eating, a dream, or what happens
when, animal-like, one feels one's body,
the centering mechanism of the body,
pulling to someone else's, magnetic, spectral,
not of this world. A small blur, a move, but
infinitesimal, like a yawn, but barely.
Like music, when you first heard it, indiscernible,
when it happens, like that.

Fragment: On the Magical World of the Animal

On my knees on the earth
and the world up above me.
Or, the world in my mind
and the trees stand around me.
I cannot see, but can hear
the dream, as it repeats
and enters the slip of my body.
With the force of a thought
or the bright smear of a dream
as it enters the sleeve of my body.
The dream of the body—what
it was, and the world:
remnant, or fragment, a thought or a thing.
The Uexküllian animal and the magical
cell-like realms of its mind.
In the dream, when it comes,
I am gone but not dead.
You are there, also, with me.
And the trees, and the film
of the world as it unspools
like a world undoing itself before us.

Hotel Letter

White dot-patterned
Wolford stockings.
Piles of makeup and glass
bottles of nail polish.

Photographs silver-duct-taped on the wall
from the studio wall in Brooklyn:
Bettina Rheims's postcard of her photograph,
"Karen Mulder with a very small Chanel bra,"
Doris Peter's "Children collecting scrap metal,
George Washington Street."

Black dress and cream blouse
with very thin black ribbon tie.
Thick denim shorts, too big, childlike.

Floradix and Magnesium.
Polaroids and magazines.

Hotel Letter

But the body,
as instrument.

A sign for something else,
but what.

In the room I am in
I listen to the static I am making
by thinking for days on end.

When I was small and electric
only the nighttime
knew me.

I made things
out of wire and some of the more delicate
trace elements.

And I made a room
inside the mind.

But the body was littler then
and I could fit
into small spaces.

When I shut my eyes,
it, too, went away.

Mornings, I walk along the abandoned airport
trying to remember what it felt like.

But the body is a mystery, a dumb
move made in childhood. Or,
made strange—the way food turns
in the hotel minibar
after too many days.

On the floor of the hotel room
are Polaroids, and ephemera:
notes I won't let go of, and photo-
graphs of who I was and what happened.

Hotel Letter

Red leather suitcase filled with Polaroid
snapshots. Or Novalis, his fragments.
What the body desires but the mind will not
allow. Or else, what the mind wants.
Language—silence and its shattered
iterations. Guyotat's desire to make
a new language was so overpowering,
by the end of 1981, he was living the creation
of his language with such obsession
he gave up eating, lost half
his body weight, and was rushed
to hospital to be resuscitated
from a coma that was nearly fatal.
On the U-Bahn at night I carry my own damage—
inside the body—inside the mind—my own self-
made language. I stop at stations based on calculations
constructed entirely on invisible patterns
of this summer's intrinsic molecular
systems. *Such language is not written down. It is
whispered into the ear at night
in a hoarse voice.* In secret,
on pink and burgundy-flocked benches
in random underground stations,
I sit in my silence and wait.

Hotel Letter

Because there are photographs—
magazines and porcelain, glitter taped
to canisters and burgundy bottles of medicine.

Hölderlin *nox animae* in the mountains of Auvergne, or
Genet in the sanctuary of his prison cell
loving the other men, tending them.

Form as the means to contain.
One wonders, what is the light that blinds,
the music that enters, then fills the body.
Rendering the mind other, black with thought.

The body as animal, a living thing, but
separate from the mind. Singing limb, or
a child not held when small,
left alone: turns, changes. You'll never recover
they said, annihilation's dark noises
will overcome you, fill you with its voices.

The summer was a flower I tended to. No,
what happened that summer
was a wound I tended to—
touched and tendered, but never nourished, never fed.

Hotel Letter

Now the poems are coming like grey rings
of memory. Or an endless series of Polaroids.
It happens like that when something happens.
And then everything changes.
I haven't slept and have taken
to walking for hours through the city
streets without destination.
It doesn't help but it does
push away the imminent tide of terror.
In the classroom I sit and watch
as the worlds move past me. And everything
is strange now. Outside the open window
are lights in the darkness, and men
linger in the chains of wetness
that occur at this hour of morning.

Hotel Letter (Refrain)

This letter I will send, though much later.
This letter or missive, disguised as a letter.
This poem, hidden inside the missive, the letter,
or poem, maybe never
dispatched. This series of photographs,
taped and kept, wound and bent, then hidden
inside the enigmatic archive. And rooms
of things: fashion magazines and bags of bright candy,
academic texts on fragments, and a ticket
roundtrip, to Warsaw or Kiev. And photographs.
Like music, it just keeps repeating,
the song. It enters the mind and then
it enters the body. Like medicine. Or,
a memory. I lost the others, you know,
the poems I wrote, but never sent.
I don't know

if those fragments or letters,
missives or caches of Polaroids
still exist, or did they
ever. In the Estonian underground
experimental film, in which
I star, as myself, but maybe
prettier and far more smarter,

I keep repeating the same ending.
What you don't ask, I can't
answer. It's obvious but still,
it's worth repeating.

Hotel Letter

In the Estonian film in which I star
as myself but prettier, or Jean Genet
when he was young in the one
black and white photograph
I have seen of him. And a room
with cameras and photographs,
piles of film and white tubes
and jars of matte, bright pink
and mint green Golden paint.
Honesty, Sabine said,
is the antidote for shame. She is
beautiful in her oversized pale-pink
sunglasses and cropped blonde hair, a bit
of Marianne Faithfull, circa 1974, mixed in.
Berlin is strange in that it exists
only in black and white. And photographs.
The trees billow like in the deep
South, but larger and more delicate,
stranger. In the prison, Genet felt more
at home, and safer. Containment
does that. I don't like him, but his calmness
masters me, he wrote. I love him
and his desire; his resistance
to self-improvement, aspiration.

He stayed what he was: orphan,
thief, hustler—and of this, he made
an intricate world, a semblance.
When I was in the hospital,
the other girls and I
changed—we became
deviant, aberrant. We morphed,
or warped. And I never
changed back.

Hotel Letter

Photographs on the wall from the studio wall in Brooklyn.
And piles of books of German literature: Hölderlin's poems,
Lenz, and Benjamin. And photographs.
On my way up my own endless mountain,
I was stopped by the triage nurse who asked me
are you female, though, are you certain. I don't know
what to think of the lovers
of my work, the letters that come to me.
I was only a child, myself, when it began.
But when the song turned to something else,
I dropped, I became something else.
Life is lived through the body but also,
hunger is an object. What will I say
when you come to me, when the darkness
has its way.

Hotel Letter

But hunger is an object, its own cellular
animal. And nourishment. What will I feed
it, how will I tend to it,
endless. In the unit
they took away my clothes, made me
put my pretty yellow Staprest slacks,
Bowie, Low, T-shirt, and silver
glitter belt in their black plastic trash bag.
It's your disease, they said.

Four times a day I sat at the long dining table
looking out over the great expanse
of nothing. Drinking vanilla and strawberry
Ensures, eating what they fed me.
Like an animal.

Fragment: Verzweiflung

In the film, Maria Schneider's
character follows Jack Nicholson's
death into the desert. In the middle
of the film, he changes, becomes
someone else. I don't know
who I am. Sabine tells me
I do, and that I confuse myself
so I can tell myself that I don't.
And whether it's something
worth pursuing or should I
just turn back. In the red car, as they drive
into the desert, she looks
back at the expanse, the beginning
of the end. Yesterday
when I saw Sabine, she said
you are empty, a vessel.
I have begun taking photographs
in an attempt to document
my every moment,
preparing. The moment
of total exhaustion
is the moment
when it all begins.

Fragment: Verwüstung

But, I have not been honest with you.
And how can you love me
if you don't know me.
Here, things are strange in that
people seem happy. Or,
the people I know: they almost died,
so now their lives are new, they have another one.
How do I say what I need to say in a poem.
I want to make this poem prettier.
If it's more beautiful, if I am
more beautiful, then
you will love me. But that, too, is a lie.
I'm better than I was, but also,
I am not: I eat normal food
but only in carefully regimented increments.
I want to be thinner, smaller.
Spectral, even. And that's a death wish,
isn't it, the death drive.
I have begun documenting
everything for an art project or maybe
something smaller, and darker.
Truth is the antidote
for shame and shame
is what I carry with me
everywhere.

Fragment

Why do I have these hands, this face
that changes everything? And where
did I misplace the letter I thought
I sent but then never could locate or replace.
Why when I read
do the words become sounds
or blocks of color or music.
In the letter I dreamt
you wrote, you told me everything.
The words broke open like words
cut from paper or collaged
onto silver metal backing,
affixed with blue duct tape,
bright pink and beige matte
paint brushed all along the back.
In the film clip in which I don't speak
but move my lips, as if whispering.

Fragment: The Earth Like a Golden Goblet Over Whose Rim the Golden Ripples of the Moon Foamed

Now the body has begun
its slow breaking down.
And still, I don't see myself.
Not like the others: beautiful
Tommy, in his pale-pink satin bomber,
his nomadic tales of illness and travel.
Sabine is trying to help me.
But, I'm tired.
This morning is a dream
I cannot wake from.
And the body is exposed,
glittering in its invisible terrors.
When I was little I sat for hours
on the dirt earth, among the animals.
Before the house, lost inside.
I had no body, then. Or,
when I shut my eyes.
But everything is changed.
I am more beautiful, sometimes,
traveling, but also nearer, more animal.

Refrain

In the one scene cut from the film
with the blonde Nina Hoss, the one in which
she is arrested and sent
to her prison of village near the sea.
On weekends, she meets her fiancé, in secret.
He arrives in the woods in a gold
Mercedes, bringing stockings
and chocolate, cigarettes and magazines.
And nights in a hotel near the sea.
Traveling, I am sometimes beautiful
but also alone and with music.
On the train to Dresden I carried
her red cosmetics case with cassettes
and records, plastic satchels of tinctures,
hypnotics and the remnants
of medicine, fractured.

Ursprung

The moment of total exhaustion
is the moment when it all begins.
Inside the large crimson and silver scrapbook
I have begun fixing images of who I really am.
In the scene in which the boy in loose black
slacks and long brown hair sits inside the parked sedan.
I am looking directly at you, into the eye
of the camera. I have begun
preparations for my final performance
titled, tentatively, "The moment of exposure,
is the moment when it all begins."
I have been trying to reach you
but all the lines are cut.
In the dream in which I keep waking,
I am trying to say something.
In the final scene
in which I do not speak,
I move my lips
as if whispering.

Fragment

Stepping off the stage,
in the middle of the set,
I was struck with its kinetics.
The body, and how what it wants
is to annihilate everything.
That it's filled with energy, and yet
when I stand before you,
my only wish is to vanish.
The body is its own
strange, and mystical language.
Genet, when I mention his name
and his years in prison,
what I mean to say is
I know I'm exposed.
What I am saying to you
in this poem can be used
against me. Not unlike the body,
how it glitters in its invisible terrors.
Or how, like the mind, the body,
ingests memory, just like how
I devour everything.
Empty vessel, I take all of it in,
so I can give you this thing.
Beautiful, sometimes, but almost

always broken, and imperfect,
this poem, this song, this fragment.

Hotel Warsaw

In a room of gold, I am
smoking.

The parade of beautiful
boys and women

have long since gone.
Along with the letters

and packets
of photographs.

Yesterday
G. read my cards:

tarot, through the white, pink
static of the television set.

Child, he said,
you are a bone.

You must leave
everything,

burn it all down
to the ground.

In the Polish black and white film
I sit inside the parked white sedan,

disguised as a boy
in oversized black slacks,

white tank, and pale-pink
satin bomber jacket.

My hair is bleached
and cropped.

I am moving
my lips as if
in a whisper.

As the camera moves nearer
I murmur

though barely,
I may be disappearing.

I am devouring
small chocolates wrapped in bright plastic.

Parked outside the high-rise
apartment

of the Warsaw
housing project.

Inside, teenage-children smoke
and carry oversized stuffed animals.

There is nothing
I would not do.

Everything I once knew,
is gone.

Fragment

G. threw my cards again this morning.
Tarot through the pale-pink
static of the Berlin Fernsehturm.
What you need is to leave,
he said. Delusion, but also
cruelty. Things are
about to turn. Everything
you love, he said,
you must first
burn down to the ground.

Hotel Letter

Piles of magazines and a suitcase
labeled danger with pamphlets
on death and transformation.

Bright plastic bags of candy,
makeup and medicine.

Like a child I roam
from room to room,
music playing in the background.

The windows of the hotel
room are cracked open
in the distance is the city's
Mercedes and Fernsehturm.

I am inside the parked sedan
outside the high-rise, waiting.

Nomadic, my entire life, I have been
packing my things and leaving.

In the hotel room
in the short black and white film,

I am the one,

the girl, the blur,
the pretty blonde
smear in the background.

Hotel Letter

By the time you read this
I will have walked off the stage
having long since lost
the words to this music.
The song is tremendous
because it has no words.
And disastrous, filled with a sweet
kind of violence. Alone in a room.
Marvelous, and it sounds just like this.
In Grünwald, Unica Zürn's father
bought her dolls that looked just like her.
He loved her because she was his.
She made a place inside her mind,
a small doll room, and inside of it
is where she lived. In Grünwald,
I ran for hours through the forest,
remembering everything.
The music and its darkness, how
its gelatinous emollient,
metallic and gorgeous,
coats the mind,
healing it back to sleep.
Contain it, I say
to her, like Genet's prisons.

Make it small, again.
And the body, wanting more,
always trying to speak,
begins its singing.

Fragment

Black coffee and bottled water
for days.

Vials of medicine,
clandestine, and expired

travel guides.
A cache of letters, unreadable

Polaroids and photographs.
Bachmann or Franza, in the desert

or, three summers ago
on a blue bus from Cairo.

My body is exposed,
glittering in its invisible skeins

of dread and terror.
And the face.

The terrible intimacy
of the mouth.

What I say
may be used against me.

Not unlike the body.
How it is always

exposed. What happened
in that house

cannot be written down.
If I have a secret

I am not telling
then I am a tomb.

Tremendous,
and without words,

the song
I am never not singing.

Fragment

But what I am
is a ghost.
Empty vessel, yet
voracious, intense.
My five-year-old self
sitting by the classroom window
replaying the same
black and white film
again and again
inside the vast coliseums
of my mind.
Sabine says, Tell your child self
that you love her.
But what I want
is to become.
Changeling, or desire.
Invisible, but with some semblance
of flower. Jean Genet
as beautiful hustler
tending the other men,
loving them. In the film
in which I star as him,
but prettier, with hidden
elements and contraband
cigarettes.

Hotel Letter

Chanel creams and training plans
for marathons. Floradix
and magnesium. Piles of glass
bottles of nail polish and a silver
cosmetics case of unused
Tom Ford makeup. When I
woke this morning I could sense
the beginning of the end.
Three months in the black flame
of the desert
and still they could not
cure my father.
You learn to live with it
I wrote once in a letter.
Black and white photographs
of Mexicans in the locked archives
of the Ethnological Museum in Berlin
and still they cannot stop
asking me where this mysterious
illness derives from.
It finally hit me
and now I have taken to smoking
cigarettes and riding the U-Bahn
to its end. Mother's Völklingen

childhood, its brilliant nebula
and yellowing opulence of iron mill,
like Ademeit's Polaroids
in which he documents each object
he owns, their milken and gaseous auras.
Sabine says, Honesty is the only
antidote for shame.
She is trying to save me.
But I am tired. And besides,
I am telling you everything.

Hotel Letter

In the letter never sent, the one
constructed entirely from photographs,
Polaroids of moments, or
elements I have been
attempting to suppress.
In this project
titled Hotel Berlin
I am writing of Hölderlin
while documenting my day-to-day
existence. I am trying to archive
the mundane details of my life,
then cut and fix them
into this poem.
But I have forgotten
nearly everything.
For instance,
what was I
before I began.
When I was small
my mother left me
in a high-rise hotel room
in Berlin. And then
she vanished.
I woke to a fire,

the windows thrown open
and a small white scar
inside the left side of my wrist.
I am pleased mostly
with the changes
and the way
I am finally
becoming.

Refrain

In the letter never sent, the one
constructed entirely of photographs.
Black coffee for breakfast with Floradix,
and Magnesium, snapshots of the path
from the apartment to the S-Bahn,
French cigarettes I bought
then finally had to throw out.
A bright blue lighter and packs
of film sealed and wrapped
in silver, baskets of berries,
museum catalogs, and Derrida's
Glas, his poetic take on Genet
and Hegel, in German
and its original, French.
In the kitchen, tins are filled
with scraps of letters and notes
collected and catalogued
to be used only in this poem.
Carmel candies, postcards
from the Ukraine and matches.
In the dream, from which I cannot wake,
I ride the train to the outskirts of the city
the high-rise, housing projects,
poverty and the children

living within it. Alone, and often
beautiful, unafraid and inside
invisible skeins and rooms,
my body, always
filling with music.

Refrain

I ride the S-Bahn out to Wedding
and don't go to class, again.
At the salon there, I dye my hair
chestnut-brown like Lispector.
Or Maria Schneider in *The Passenger*.
Then, I leave my clothes and everything
I own. It is death, and its needle,
I am thinking of. Bachmann, or Franza,
in Egypt, and her escape
from her husband, his fascism,
and the sanitarium he forced her into.
My father, when I was fifteen, was sent
into the desert. He went missing
and I didn't think
I would ever see him again.
When he came back, he was not
the same man. Changing,
the poems are becoming
letters or songs.
Making them is all I do.
That, and the endless photographs.
And I am trying not to want
to be someone else, or myself,
but better, which is, in a sense,

a kind of death
drive, a death wish.
The body and language
and their eventual collision
is what I am banking on.
The children here,
in Berlin, where I am,
their eyes are wild
and when they run,
their bodies are young
and not yet owned
by anyone.

Fragment

Polaroids of photographs and stacks
of books and magazines
and Polaroids. Warburg,
and his texts filled with black and white
photographs of his time in the desert.
What became, later,
evidence of his sanity and
freedom from Binswanger's asylum.
Let the poem write you, Sabine
says. But this poem is for Doris
in Völklingen, and the black and white photographs
of her blonde-white childhood.
In ironed cotton dress in the glittering
soot of that iron-town.
And I am trying not to become
someone else. Not to evoke
Tina Chow in her final moments
in the Pacific Palisades, in the
quarantine ward of the hospital.
And those Polaroids. Tinctures
and teas, and how they could not
save her. I wanted to be something
else. Myself, but better. Wild,
and not-yet, a burn, maybe
as it is occurring.

Phosphorescence

Photographs of photographs and Polaroids
of stacks of books on fragments
and photographs and pamphlets
on letters sent and imminent
collisions. What the body does not know
it wants. And the mind.
In the song I wrote
I said I wanted to be
like you, but then
I pulled back.
I am afraid most of the time
of my own intensity.
Not its kinesis, its brilliant light
and energy, but that it might
frighten you.
I have tried my whole life
to contain it, hold it
back. Make myself
into the perfect song,
the most contained
poem. But now I am
letting go of all of that.
I have taken to photographing
my every moment

in an attempt to locate
the place where I lost myself.
When the body and the mind conflate
or, rather, when the body and language.
That is the moment I have been waiting for.

Fragment

The beautiful travelers
on the train
this morning.

And the letter
from S., and his
breaking.

He was speaking
he says,
his entire life,

from inside
the prison
of his own body.

Without ever once
opening
his mouth.

But what is the body
but language,
untamed?

And what is this music—

The Moment of Exposure Is the Moment When It All Begins

In the German film, in the scene in which
the blonde actress who plays Gudrun Ensslin,
sits smoking in a miniskirt in her parents' house,
watching footage of the police assassination
of Benno Ohnesorg. You can see her body
filling with music, with the energy of the moment.
And the black and white images
inside the static of the television set.
How their bodies are filled with energy,
a kind of uncurbed kinesis or frenetic
music. In the scene before she leaves,
changing her life completely. In the film
in which I star as her, but alone, in my own
apartment. I sit listening to the static
of the radio. And piles of photographs
and magazines with images of men in black,
their bodies moving across the screen,
their bodies filling with an untamable
music. *Someone, you or me,*
comes forward and says:
I would like to learn to live, finally.

Fragment

So this is twilight.

What holds
this moment together.

When in the film, in which
I star as myself,

I say I want to be you,

what I mean is
I want to know
what it feels like.

There comes a moment,
I was warned,
when all the signs collide,

everything I have ever learned
converges.

I woke in that blindness
this morning.

The photographs I have been taking
I don't want to show them
not to anyone.

I am too much
exposed and afraid

of what might happen
in that moment.

Fragment

What happens in that moment,
that flash of phosphorescence.

Like sleep, when light's
semblance enters.

The way a dream
enters the sleeve of the body.

I am trying
to archive this moment.

Gather, collect, and keep
every disparate thing
that lives within it.

But each time
I move near—

the elements,
and then the trace,
vanishes.

Who are you.

And what language.

What body, and what
strange series of syllables

is that
speaking through you.

The Gift

This poem
is a hospital.

A bed near a window,
and a lamp.

Fractured and dissonant,
the music it emits.

The sound
of the precise hours

I traveled

in Berlin,
on the U-Bahn.

Taking in
the bodies of strangers,
loving them.

Here, then, is its medicine.

Spectral, and archived,
the one moment in time.

Milky, and overexposed,
the black and white photograph
in which you move your body,
slow, into the room

in which everything
you have ever known
exists, still, dream-like
and alive.

This poem, this photograph
or archive, this bend
in the moment,

—waiting only
for you.

Fragment: I Twice Drew, Both Times from a Different Angle, the Gap Between Two Poplar Trees

Black and white photographs
torn from the pages of magazines
from the 1970s. And stacks of books
and artifacts on movement theory
and the work of the post-conceptual
artists of the former Eastern bloc.
Small, seemingly mundane actions
such as the washing of one's own face,
in the isolation of one's own home
do, in fact, count as acts of art.
Or, rather, as valid means of protest.
In a society in which the state is everywhere
and sees all. In a culture in which
everything is swallowed and then
refashioned, what constitutes as
nourishment. For three years
I traveled from city to city,
at work on a performance
piece titled, "Hotel Rooms" in which
I lived for one month increments
in Warsaw, Berlin, and Belgrade.
Containment is often detrimental.
And I have spent my life trying
in as many ways as I can

to escape it. But some type of containment
is needed. Genet was happiest in prison
and it was there with the other men
that he could love entirely, be
who he was without terror
of exposure. In the hotel rooms,
I photographed myself
performing small gestures such as
the act of drinking tea or the ritual
of smearing rose water on the face
when waking, after a bath.
In the embrace of isolation
and the reduction of artistic means,
in that small and nearly silent
opening, that minute movement—
it is there, in that increment,
where, finally, the promise
of a new language will appear.

Fragment: Warsaw

. . . the structure of the archive is *spectral.*
—Derrida, *Archive Fever*

But the world wants us dead.

I wrote once in a poem or a letter I wrote
but never sent.

On the slow train to Kiev, Warsaw,
or Belgrade.

High-rise housing projects
inside a silence

I can't remember
where from.

Hotel Belgrade

In Belgrade in my hotel room
I return to the self-portraits
from the earlier work:

smoking in the tub
while reading
texts on the New Art Practice.

When I step out of the bathroom
and into the music
with no witness
it still happens.

And when I whisper
into the soft crimson leather
back seat of the parked sedan,
I still exist.

I am here
even when you do not
see me.

I am here
because I say
that I am.

Fragment

Reverie of the esoteric
German film in which
I star as the blonde actress
who plays the daughter
of a Protestant, turned militant.
In black smudged eyeliner
reading incendiary texts
in a porcelain tub, smoking.
When you entered the room
I was riveted by the energy
of the moment, and its kinesis,
the athletic frenetics of it.
A sweet kind of violence: desire
when it finally enters the body.

Correspondence

Drowsed in crimson and sun-bleached
flowers, in bright pink glitter, black and silver
swimsuit. Glistening cream buckles,
butter leather Mercedes back seat.
In the montage-collage of myriad
experiences: the tiny chapel in Prague
and opaque Warsaw skyline, the pool
at the roof of the Intercontinental,
I pasted you back
into the pretty discotheque-
like diorama I had been working on.
One hand on my Fiskar scissors,
another on the precious blue-paste,
or child-style, Uhu. What was left
from the boxes I brought back
from my brother's enormous flat
in the former East, Berlin.
And the plastic-wrapped
EP records I'd kept
from that strange phase of when.
Athletic, I have always been
a strange, always hungry, animal.
Sleeping in the back seats of parked sedans
and, speaking by not, by pasting

one image next to the other,
a slideshow, a montage of
bright photographs doing the work
that words cannot.

Fragment

When we crossed over the border
I wasn't sure, anymore.
My mind was filling with so much music.
It all went white, then black.
The men who checked our passes
and asked for our assurances
vanished when I asked.
Who are you. And what
strange and beautiful music.
In part two of the film,
the scene in which I can't
rise from the bed.

The Undersong

But whose voice will enter
and what will I do
with that brutal but beautiful music.
In the city, from my hotel window
I can see the elements and trace.
Structures constructed to protect the mind
and the gorgeous culture of the body.
In the park nearby, at dusk.
With plastic transistor radio
and magnetic apparatus,
so small they fit into the palm
of my hand.

Fragment

I would like this poem
to be a machine.
Concise, metallic,
a counting apparatus.
A means to keep each moment
contained and fixed, akin
to a series of Polaroids,
photographed and fixed
to cardboard or some other
paper panel backing.
Then photographed and affixed
with scotch tape to the wall.
Or, a vitrine, a glass case,
within which to gather and collect
each moment, each object
representing each moment.
A bundle, assemblage, or archive
constructed of letters and notes,
diary entries and fragments,
articles and photographs
torn from books.
A machine that measures
the space between
the body and the mind,

the dissonance that exists
inside that moment. And there,
in that static, in the rip,
the mar, the error
between, is where,
when it begins, it will
begin.

Hotel Warsaw: Fragment

. . . for my body does not have the same ideas I do.
—Roland Barthes, *The Pleasure of the Text*

In the hotel room are stacks of magazines
and texts on photography, platters of food
and snapshots of the black and white photographs
of the montage work of the Romanian artist
whose work documents the space between.
I want to know that language.
I want to live inside it.
And I want my body
to lead me, not the mind.
But the body, it wants
to devour everything.
For instance, last night I swallowed
chocolate after chocolate
inside the hotel tub, while reading.
What the body wants
and the mind does not.
But the mind, it will not quit.
And still, I cannot stop
feeding it. Or the body,
its animal-like desire,
its dumb and blind
collisions, with everything.

Philosophy

In the German film in which
I am disguised as the blonde actress
who portrays the activist turned anarchist,
I am wearing a blonde wig,
disguised as a German film actress.
When I was sixteen I lived
in an abandoned house
with other young anarchists.
We lived inside a small dream
in which we lived
with each other
inside a kind of sweet dream.
But then the boys turned
to heroin and then to ways
of making money to pay for it.
When I asked, they would not say.
But you can see shame and sorrow
when it appears in the face.
I loved them
but by then there was nothing left
of who they had been.
By the time I left
most of them were dead.
I don't know

what to do with this passion.
It wants things I know
I can't handle. But the opposite
is a passive death I cannot accept.
When in the film, the actress
is finally hunted down and sent to prison,
she lives inside her cell
reading and listening to news
of the world on her transistor radio.
Living a kind of death
I know already
all too well.

The Way

But, I don't understand
anything. And I am trying
hard not to. What the world
wanted, what it wanted of me.
But underwater, I like the way
my body looks when swimming
in summer, and alone. An amber blur,
like music when it enters the unexpecting
body. Unfathomable, an energy.
Or static coming off the satellite
radio late at night
from a distant, foreign city.
When I was little I wanted
to be famous. Beautiful, an actress,
maybe. That was before I knew
things. And now sometimes I want
nothing but to run for hours
through the forest,
inside the deep silence
of my own body
and its mind.

Small Atlas

In the action slash happening
based on the earlier performance work
by the Hungarians, Miklós Erdély and Dóra
Maurer, I am disguised
as a French actress
whose only known appearance
was as an activist in a film never
made by the little-known director
who, after the script was lost, vanished.
Shot entirely by handheld camera
inside a hotel room in West Berlin,
the film is based loosely
on the anti-psychiatry movement
that occurred during the May 1968 French uprisings.
I am tired, she wrote
to Foucault, before she vanished
somewhere in the Egyptian desert.
Or, in Rome, in a hotel room,
smoking cigarette after cigarette and drinking
to excess in a final futile attempt
to archive the detritus and remnants
of a culture she was no longer able
to comprehend. When I step backwards
onto the stage I am wearing a short blonde wig

and nothing but strong makeup and undergarments.
I mouth the words
of Marguerite Duras,
months before her death.
Somewhat missing
from the place where I am speaking.
She wrote these words
in her final text titled, *No*
More. In a stupor, already
consumed by death.
I am living inside a prison
of my own making,
the female producer confessed
in a rare interview aired just once
late at night, on Radio France.
And I have begun now to imagine
what it might be like
to make art entirely
in solitude, to finally
enter the work, and become
what I have been for so many years
afraid of: the space between, the place
of magnificent, though, mostly
terrifying, silence.

Tagebücher

I cancelled everything yesterday
and caught the U-Bahn to Prenzlauer Berg
where the actor or model or maybe
musician featured in the black and white film
titled *Nocturnal*, cut my hair.
Stripped and bleached it
the color of wheat or a small child's.
His long thin arms and neck
were covered in black and green ink
and the name of a man or a woman
drawn in cursive on the side of his childlike face.
It hurts, sometimes, to walk through all of this.
But mostly I know I am not alone.
I don't know where you came from,
even less—what will happen.
Before the mirror, I was changed.
He made me what I was
to begin with: sometimes
beautiful and somewhat
childlike. Always,
not one thing, but many.
Where it all collides
in its montage or archive.
Frenetic, in energy and relentless.

A series of Polaroid photographs,
clips from forgotten esoteric
films and long abandoned texts.
A poem, unfolding,
right here, before you.

Hotel Letter

Stacks of texts on the black and white
photographs of Miklós Erdély and his
short films and happenings.
And Polaroids of moments
caught by camera. Photographed,
then fixed to the walls with glue and blue
packing tape. By capturing each moment
and each object carrying each moment
I thought I might finally unpack
the blacked-out memory.
Preverbal, visceral, fixed
inside a music I can hear only
inside my own body.
When I was fifteen I caught the bus
into the city every week for singing
lessons. But when I stood before
the teacher's mirrors, I'd lose
the words, and then the music.
I don't know how to unpack it,
or how to place the objects
back into their gold light.
Where is the essence from which
music and desire originate.
And how do I return to that.

Felt

Dresden is halfway to Prague
and Prague is halfway to Kiev.
But Kiev is halfway to Lvov
or Lviv, which is where
my grandfather's father
comes from. I don't know what
he left when he left that city
or, what occurred to him
within himself, when he was made
to change his name. I don't know
where he came from,
the man I met on the train,
or what his name was.
But we sat in strict silence
for hours so that
when we arrived in the Ukraine
I felt I genuinely knew him.
What is the porcelain light
that exists inside silence.
And how were we able
to swallow and then enter
its warm and subtle bells
at the entrance to that

one majestic and yet
slightly chemical
night.

Fragment: Nachleben

In the black and white Polish film
in which the beautiful local
plays the nun. In Warsaw,
she meets her aunt, once powerful,
now alcoholic, who directs her to her
true past. I am struggling with understanding
unsure which past is mine.
In the film in the scene
where the actress wears her dead
aunt's dress and heels
after the aunt has killed herself.
I am inside that moment,
the split in the seam
in which almost anything can happen.
When she drinks the liquor
the world falls opens,
as when she hears the music
playing rooms away.
I don't know what future
or past, or whose film role
I should step into.
I only know the body is not
what I thought. And the mind
is just a dumb machine

that makes small traces.
In the film in the scene in which
the actress returns to the convent
and the camera pulls away.
There is a rip, a mar,
an error that occurs,
but only off screen.
That break, that space
between, is the moment
when it all begins.

Correspondence

At dawn, after they drove me
by emergency to the hospital,
or the mansion on the outskirts of the city.
Through the bleached fields
and positioned on the silver hillside.
To be alone doesn't hurt that much
he wrote, in that poem
he wrote before he died.
After Trakl, and the translations of his writings
in which he writes of his own alienation.
Sebastian in Dream and his mother's compulsions:
filling their Viennese home with opulent objects
so that there is no room left
for her children. *In a dream,*
the wanderer goes. My father,
when I was small, promised me
a shetland pony for my courage
after we moved, again. But then,
we moved again. From city to city.
Nomads, with no home. To live inside
one's mind, is its own locked hotel room,
its own phantasm and cell. Its own
strange poem. Genet in his prisons,
loving the men, tending to them.

Strangers in hotel rooms reading my tarot,

begging me to touch them.

In Prague and Warsaw,

dreaming in Latin, with my hands.

Schöna

You are an empty vessel,
Sabine says. So take everything in.
But how do I make myself vacant.
Outside the city of Dresden
the mountains are miraculous
in that they exist as strange
but beautiful chalk-like formations.
They arise from no place
like an apparition. How do I know
what is real and what is not
I asked her and she said, You
tell yourself you don't know
to confuse yourself. But you do.
Wittgenstein, perhaps due to his family
and their vast cruelties,
spent his entire life trying
to find the perfect equation,
truth as a numerical solution.
A poem is alchemical
like magic or tarot.
In other words, the words
in this poem are performative.
What I say to you, in this poem,
will happen, is happening,

as I say the words. After today,
I am only an empty vessel.
A series of glass vitrines, endless
rooms, or an emptied out
archive. I will take everything in.
Collect, and contain, devour and swallow
every single bell of light and all
of your trembling cells of sorrow.
Here, even, now you can try it:
open your mouth
and feed me your vowels,
sweet in their magnificence,
radical and terrible.
Watch as I transform, then vanish
before you.

The Reason

In Prague, in the church of the holy
spirit, a hidden record player
is playing Turandot. On the low
stage are two pale-pink chairs,
a microphone stand and, at the edge,
a crimson velvet curtain.
When the non-actress who plays
the nun in Paweł Pawlikowski's film
Ida, hears the music playing
from her small hotel room,
she is drawn to the small stage
near the bar, two stories down.
Off camera, she watches the band,
mesmerized. As the music enters
her body, she is changed. On the stage
a beautiful woman is singing.
She is the other version of the nun
whose name is Wanda, but whose
real name is Ida. Her aunt is another
double, one more version of who
she might become. In the black
and white photograph of Edie
Sedgwick in The Factory, the one
where she is staring directly

into the camera. It is in her eyes
that you see it—desire and its
blinding ravishment.
It is beautiful but it has death
inside it. She escaped California
and the cruelty of her family
but she carried its brutal music
with her everywhere she went.
It is as if she knows already
precisely what will happen.
What love lays bare in me,
Barthes wrote, is energy.
What is this energy for, I asked
Sabine, the last time I saw her.
It is this energy, silent, and smoldering
childlike in its language—
that is the only reason
for my being here.

The Language

Silent and smoldering, the language
and only reason for my being here,
I said to Sabine the last time I saw her.
Present the worst, the most
embarrassing work, she said.
Then add stronger work around it.
Remember, she said, you are an empty
vessel. And intense, you feel everything.
too much. I have been practicing, now,
presenting the most humiliating.
Without context, with no explanation.
Allowing the world to create its own
conclusion. It is terrifying, and I am afraid
what the world will do. But also
it is a kind of abyss. An ending.
Eva Hesse, when she returned
to Germany with her husband,
realized he did not see her.
She had a breakthrough then,
when walking, she saw the remnants
of that culture: plastic and metal
wire, glass and other forms of what
others considered waste and garbage.
And she began to work with these

terrible materials and chemicals.
Present the worst, the weakest,
most powerfully vulnerable work.
Life doesn't last; art doesn't last.
It doesn't matter, Hesse said later,
near her death, in an interview.
What matters is the trace. Silent,
the willingly weak and near-
incoherent language, inside.

Fragment: With Scrap of Fur on My Left Shoulder

Unburdened, I am free now
to enter it: the terrible and feral music.
When I rode into the Egyptian desert
on my way to Saint Catherine's
I was thinking of Anne Marie
Schwarzenbach, her repeated travels
by car to Persia, Afghanistan,
Russia, and the Balkans.
Compulsive, and often
accompanied by morphine.
In Berlin, with the Manns, then later,
with others. Consumed by desire.
In Marriane Breslauer's black and white
photograph in which Schwarzenbach
stares directly into the camera.
Her immense sorrow is evident
in the eyes, dark with sorrow.
And though thoroughly composed,
in men's shirt and wool sweater,
she looks lost. Father says
I have been asleep since he first knew me.
You are half awake, not alive, he said.
But what does it take, and how
does one get there?

Hotel Nocturnal

In the black and white photograph
I am standing in the background.
What you see is a blur and my face,
slowly turning. I am watching the low stage
before me. I am standing behind the boy
gazing into the gutter of the photograph.
I don't know him. But his body
is filling slowly with light. His gaze
is aimed at something
not inside the room.
I want to know where desire
comes from, and what is it
made of. Death, but also
something that is still alive
and childlike. His face is radiant
with longing. But, also sorrow.
He knows he cannot have
what he wants. Or that
what he desires might destroy him.
I am alone most of the time
but sometimes beautiful,
unafraid and with music.

Bambule

In the German film in which I play
the German intellectual turned militant.
I am smoking again, waiting
impatiently at my desk by the window.
I am reading Gramsci and listening
to news of the world from my beautiful
black metallic transistor radio.
When I was young I was not loved
by anyone. And that experience
is what formed me, made me
what I am. Empty, a vessel,
but also, I feel everything
too much. In the blue house
with the other beautiful delinquents.
And later, with the other almost-girls,
all of us hungry, always, for something
other than what we were
being given. When, in the film,
I leave everything behind,
it doesn't feel like anything.
The cut that was made in me
was made when I was small.
Everything that happened, after,
was just play acting.

The Moment

Ulrike Meinhof's film, *Bambule*
or *Riot*, made for German television
but pulled before it was aired.
In the first scene as the two girls
are attempting to run away, the blonde
actress is caught on camera, her face
changed, in a moment of stark
realization. There is no escape
or, there is no place to escape to.
The detention center they are imprisoned in
is a mere microcosm. The system is intricate
and more brilliant than we are.
In the black and white film clip
her beautiful face is frozen
and her eyes are closed.
The moment is a tiny death
that exists inside the film
shot. And in it, she is also
trapped. In prison, Meinhof and her comrade,
Gudrun Ensslin, ordered texts
written by the philosopher Wittgenstein.
They were trying, it seems,
to find a new language.
In Gerhard Richter's

paintings of the black and white
photographs of Ensslin taken in prison.
She is frozen in a series of death
masks, invisible to her but evident
in the snapshots.
I don't know what to do
with this passion. It wants
what I know I cannot handle.
But the opposite is a listlessness,
a drug-like torpor.
In the fall I will meet
with Father again
and he will remind me.

Definition

Home I ask, What is it.

Magnificent, a small death
with frenetic noise and music.
A dropping down into, an absolution.

You confuse yourself, Sabine says,
You tell yourself you don't know, but you do.

Its Origins

I didn't want to look
to see the thing I made.
I knew if I did, the shame
would enter back into me
like a song that won't stop
repeating. I was confined
inside the narrow space. But I was
using my arms, my strength.
Remember, she said, shame is a veil
milky like film or the upper
layer of dreams. You can lift it
with your fingers, using your substance.
But the mind is a machine. It never stops
thinking. In the photograph
I am wearing a scarf of many small
bright birds and the silver
branches of unknown trees.
I am moving against the future,
my small body pushed up
against its glass.

NOTES

The title "Blood Work—Steady Decline" is from the series "Untitled" (21 Days of Bloodwork—Steady Decline) (1994) by the artist Felix Gonzalez-Torres.

In "Fragment: Pollen," the word "pollen" in the poem's title derives from Novalis's text of philosophical and poetic fragments originally titled *Pollen*.

In "Hotel Letter (Red leather suitcase filled with Polaroid)" "Such language is not written down. It is whispered into the ear at night in a hoarse voice. At dawn it is forgotten" is from *The Thief's Journal* by Jean Genet.

The poem "Fragment: On the Magical World of the Animal" is informed by the zoologist, Jakob von Uexküll's, *A Foray into the Worlds of Animals and Humans: With a Theory of Meaning.*

In "Hotel Letter" (Photographs on the wall from the studio wall in Brooklyn)" the phrase "Hunger is an object" comes from Herta Müller's novel *The Hunger Angel.*

In "Fragment (In the film, Maria Schneider's)," "Fragment (In the short black and white film), and "The Moment of Exposure is the Moment When it All Begins" the line, "The moment of total exhaustion is the moment when it all begins" comes from Stephen Barber's essay, "On the Road with Pierre Guyotat" included in his text *Pierre Guyotat: Revolutions & Aberrations.*

In "Fragment: The Earth Like a Golden Goblet Over Whose Rim the Golden Ripples of the Moon Foamed," "Fragment (Black coffee and bottled water)," and "Fragment (Stepping off the stage)" the phrase "The body is exposed glittering in its invisible terrors" and variations thereof, originate in Jean Genet's *The Thief's Journal*.

In "Fragment: The Earth Like a Golden Goblet Over Whose Rim the Golden Ripples of the Moon Foamed" the phrase "The Earth Like a Golden Goblet Over Whose Rim the Golden Ripples of the Moon Foamed" is from Georg Büchner's novella fragment, *Lenz*.

The line "Someone, you or me comes forward and says: I would like to learn to live, finally" in the poem "The Moment of Total Exposure is the Moment When it All Begins" is from an interview with Jacques Derrida from *Derrida: Learning to Live Finally. The Last Interview.*

In the poem, "Fragment: I Twice Drew, Both Times from a Different Angle, the Gap Between Two Poplar Trees" the title comes from the Czech Action artist, Milan Maur's, action titled, "On April 20, 1987 in Plzeň-Lobzy, I twice drew, both times from a different angle, the gap between two poplar trees."

The phrase, "with scrap of fur on my left shoulder" in the poem title, "Fragment: With Scrap of fur on My Left Shoulder" is from Georg Büchner's novella fragment, *Lenz*. The original reads, "with scrap of fur on his left shoulder."

In the poem "Fragment: (Black coffee and bottled water)" "If I have a secret I am not telling then I am a tomb" is from Hélène Cixous's "If we have a secret we don't tell then we truly are a tomb" from *Three Steps on the Ladder of Writing*.

Acknowledgments

The following poems have been published in various iterations in the following journals:

The Baffler, Bear Review, Bomb Magazine, Changes Review, Columbia Journal, Dizzy, Elke, Field, Goliad, Gulf Coast, Hermeneutic Chaos, The Journal, Jubiliat, Jung Journal: Culture and Psyche, La Vague, Little Brown Mushroom Newsletter, Neck Press Review, Ocean State Review, Paris Review, Periodicities: A Journal of Poetry and Poetics, Poor Claudia, Prairie Schooner, Plume, Southeast Review, Speakeasy Anthology, Thrush, Two Peach, Washington Square Review, and *Zocalo Public Square.*

Cruz is the author of six collections of poems: *Guidebooks for the Dead* (Four Way Books, 2020), *Dregs* (Four Way Books, 2018), *How the End Begins* (Four Way Books, 2016), *Wunderkammer* (Four Way Books, 2014), *The Glimmering Room* (Four Way Books, 2012) and *Ruin* (Alice James Books, 2006). *Disquieting: Essays on Silence*, a collection of critical essays exploring the concept of silence as a form of resistance, was published by Book*hug in the spring of 2019. *The Melancholia of Class: A Manifesto for the Working Class*, an exploration of melancholia and the working class, was published by Repeater Books in July of 2021.

Cruz earned an MA in German Language and Literature from Rutgers University and is currently pursuing a PhD at the European Graduate School where her area of research is psychoanalysis and philosophy. Cruz teaches in the Graduate Writing Program at Columbia University and is a visiting writer in the MFA Writing Program at the University of Massachusetts, Amherst. She is also a mentor in the Low Residency MFA Writing Program at the Institute of American Indian Arts. Cruz co-edits the multidisciplinary online journal, *Schlag Magazine*.

Publication of this book was made possible by grants and donations. We are also grateful to those individuals who participated in our 2021 Build a Book Program. They are:

Anonymous (16), Maggie Anderson, Susan Kay Anderson, Kristina Andersson, Kate Angus, Kathy Aponick, Sarah Audsley, Jean Ball, Sally Ball, Clayre Benzadón, Greg Blaine, Laurel Blossom, Adam Bohannon, Betsy Bonner, Lee Briccetti, Joan Bright, Jane Martha Brox, Susan Buttenwieser, Anthony Cappo, Carla and Steven Carlson, Paul and Brandy Carlson, Renee Carlson, Alice Christian, Karen Rhodes Clarke, Mari Coates, Jane Cooper, Ellen Cosgrove, Peter Coyote, Robin Davidson, Kwame Dawes, Michael Anna de Armas, Brian Komei Dempster, Renko and Stuart Dempster, Matthew DeNichilo, Rosalynde Vas Dias, Kent Dixon, Patrick Donnelly, Lynn Emanuel, Blas Falconer, Elliot Figman, Jennifer Franklin, Helen Fremont and Donna Thagard, Gabriel Fried, John Gallaher, Reginald Gibbons, Jason Gifford, Jean and Jay Glassman, Dorothy Tapper Goldman, Sarah Gorham and Jeffrey Skinner, Lauri Grossman, Julia Guez, Sarah Gund, Naomi Guttman and Jonathan Mead, Kimiko Hahn, Mary Stewart Hammond, Beth Harrison, Jeffrey Harrison, Melanie S. Hatter, Tom Healy and Fred Hochberg, K.T. Herr, Karen Hildebrand, Joel Hinman, Deming Holleran, Lillian Howan, Thomas and Autumn Howard, Catherine Hoyser, Elizabeth Jackson, Jessica Jacobs and Nickole Brown, Christopher Johanson, Jen Just, Maeve Kinkead, Alexandra Knox, Lindsay and John Landes, Suzanne Langlois, Laura Lauth, Sydney Lea, David Lee and Jamila Trindle, Rodney Terich Leonard, Jen Levitt, Howard Levy, Owen Lewis, Matthew Lippman, Jennifer Litt, Karen Llagas, Sara London and Dean Albarelli, Clarissa Long, James Longenbach, Cynthia Lowen, Ralph and Mary Ann Lowen, Ricardo Maldonado, Myra Malkin, Jacquelyn Malone, Carrie Mar, Kathleen McCoy, Ellen McCulloch-Lovell, Lupe Mendez, David Miller, Josephine Miller, Nicki Moore, Guna Mundheim, Matthew Murphy and Maura Rockcastle, Michael and Nancy Murphy, Myra Natter, Jay Baron Nicorvo, Ashley Nissler, Kimberly Nunes, Rebecca and Daniel Okrent, Robert Oldshue and Nina Calabresi, Kathleen Ossip, Judith Pacht, Cathy McArthur Palermo, Marcia and Chris Pelletiere, Sam Perkins, Susan Peters and Morgan Driscoll, Patrick Phillips, Robert Pinsky, Megan Pinto, Connie Post, Kyle Potvin, Grace Prasad, Kevin Prufer, Alicia Jo Rabins, Anna Duke Reach, Victoria Redel, Martha Rhodes, Paula Rhodes, Louise Riemer, Sarah Santner, Amy Schiffman, Peter and Jill Schireson, Roni and Richard Schotter, James and Nancy Shalek, Soraya Shalforoosh, Peggy Shinner, Anita Soos,

Donna Spruijt-Metz, Ann F. Stanford, Arlene Stang, Page Hill Starzinger, Marina Stuart, Yerra Sugarman, Marjorie and Lew Tesser, Eleanor Thomas, Tom Thompson and Miranda Field, James Tjoa, Ellen Bryant Voigt, Connie Voisine, Moira Walsh, Ellen Dore Watson, Calvin Wei, John Wender, Eleanor Wilner, Mary Wolf, and Pamela and Kelly Yenser.